Learn to Read Persian (Farsi) in 5 Days

DAVOUD TURANI

CONTENTS

INTRODUCTION

Learning a new alphabet can be very intimidating for an English speaker only used to reading the Latin alphabet. This is partly why English speakers tend to stick to learning other languages that use the same alphabet, such as French, Spanish and Italian – because they seem a lot easier!

But learning a new alphabet does not have to be so difficult. The difficulty is finding a good system to learn the new alphabet so that the student does not get discouraged and give up before making any real progress. Making progress in the language is the best motivator.

The secret to learning a new alphabet is to be taught each letter separately, and then to practice how the new letters combine with letters you already know to read real words in the language in a structured way. This is not revolutionary – it is probably how you learned to read English – but it is not easy to find for other languages.

This book will teach you how to read the Persian (Farsi) alphabet in exactly that way, and with this method you will be able to read Persian in only 5 days or less! After that you will be able to enjoy the Persian language and culture in a way that you were never able to before

THE PERSIAN ALPHABET
الفبای فارسی

The Persian alphabet contains 32 letters and is written from right to left, the opposite direction of English. The script is a modification of the Arabic alphabet, with four new letters added to represent sounds that do not exist in Arabic. The Persian alphabet does not contain different upper and lowercase letters. However, the Persian alphabet is exclusively written cursively. This means that letters slightly change shape in order to connect to the previous and following letters in a word, similar to English cursive handwriting. This cursive character is always maintained, even on computers; when one types letters in the Persian alphabet, the software joins the letters together. Letters are never allowed to be left unconnected.

One noticeable feature of the Persian alphabet is that several different letters are pronounced identically. This is because the Arabic alphabet used to write Persian has many letters that represent sounds that do not exist in Persian. When Arabic loanwords, of which the Persian language has many, are written in Persian they retain the Arabic spelling but are pronounced using different sounds. For example, Persian has four letters that are all pronounced with a "z" sound!

Like the alphabet used to write Arabic, vowels are not usually written in Persian, although some consonants are used to represent long vowels. A system does exist to fully spell out the short vowels as a series of dashes and lines above and below the word. The vowel markings are only used in certain texts, however, such as religious texts and books for children, and are not seen in most publications. For this reason they are not included in this book.

The lack of written vowels makes the Persian alphabet somewhat challenging for beginners, since it is not always clear exactly how to pronounce a word one sees written. However, much like Modern English with its weird spellings, once you develop a feel for the language, it is actually not at all as difficult as it seems at first.

HOW TO USE THIS COURSE

The primary goal of this course book is to teach the reader to recognize the Persian alphabet and to begin to read the Persian language.

The main way this is accomplished is by teaching the individual pronunciations of each letter, and then utilizing "Practice" sections where the student can practice reading real Persian words. These "Practice" sections are very important and the main way the student will start to feel comfortable with the Persian alphabet. The answers to all "Practice" questions are included directly below the questions, but try to avoid looking at the answers until you have attempted to answer the questions yourself.

Throughout the book, the reader will also learn approximately 150 real Persian words. These words have been carefully selected to be of maximum benefit to beginner students of the language and are a great starting point for students who want to continue their study of Persian. In the end of the book there are two glossaries – one in thematic order and one in alphabetical order – where the student can study and memorize all the words learned in this course.

The course material has been designed to be completed slowly over five days, while reviewing lessons as necessary. You are encouraged to go at whatever pace you feel comfortable with and to feel free to go back to lessons to review as much as needed.

Good luck and I hope you enjoy the first step on your journey to learning the Persian language.

UNIT 1 - ب, ک, م, د

The first letter introduced in this course is the Persian letter ب.
This letter is pronounced like the "b" sound in "boy" (IPA: /b/).
Persian is a cursive script and most letters change shape slightly in
order to join to the surrounding letters. The letter ب has four
different forms, isolated, initial, medial and final, depending on its
place in the word; these forms are (from right to left):

ب ب ـبـ ـب

Note that although the shape of the letter changes, the single dot
below the letter stays the same. These dots are crucial in Persian
and the main way to distinguish letters.

The letter ک is pronounced like the "k" sound in "kite" (IPA: /k/).
Like ب, ک changes shape depending on its place in the word. The
isolated, initial, medial and final forms are:

ک کـ ـکـ ـک

The letter م is pronounced like the English "m" in "mother" or
"Mary" (IPA: /m/). Like the two letters above, م has four forms:

م مـ ـمـ ـم

The last letter of this unit is the letter د, which is pronounced like
the English "d" sound in "dad" (IPA: /d/). There are two types of
letters in Persian with respect to how they join with other letters.
The first three letters in the unit, ب, ک, and م have four different
forms because they join to the previous and following letters. The
other type has only two forms because it never joins to the letter
that follows it. The letter د is the second type. The two forms of
this letter (isolated and final) are:

د ـد

1

PRACTICE

Try to recognize these English words in their Persian disguises. Remember that Persian is written from right to left and short vowels are not written. The answers are below.

1. بد
2. بک
3. دب
4. دم
5. مد
6. دک

ANSWERS

1. bad (or bed)
2. back
3. dab
4. dam
5. mad
6. deck

UNIT 2 - ا, آ, ت, ن

When a word starts with a vowel sound in Persian, that vowel is written with a ا regardless of the vowel. Beginners can assume a short "a" sound when this letter begins a word, but remember that in some cases it could also be a short "o" sound or an "e" sound and only consulting a native speaker or a dictionary will confirm.

There are two separate "a" sounds in the Persian language. One is the short "a" sound in "cat" (IPA: /æ/) and the other is the long "a" sound in "father" or even like saying "aww" at the dentist (IPA: /ɒ/). It is important to not confuse these two "a" sounds as the wrong "a" sound can change the meaning of a word.

When the letter ا is written in the middle or end of a word, it is always the long "a" sound. The long "a" sound will be represented in the pronunciation of this book with â. Remember that the short "a" sound in the middle of a word is not written. ا has only two forms since it can only connect to the previous letter:

ا ﺍ

At the beginning of a word, in order to distinguish the long and short "a" sounds, the long "a" sound is always written آ.

The letter ت is pronounced like the "t" sound in "ten" or "Tom" (IPA: /t/). ت has the following four forms depending on its position in the word:

ﺕ ﺗ ﺘ ﺖ

The letter ن is pronounced like the "n" sound in "now" (IPA: /n/). ن has the following four forms depending on its position in the word:

ﻥ ﻧ ﻨ ﻦ

TRY NOT TO CONFUSE

The letters ب, ت, and ن have the same basic shape in all of their forms and are therefore distinguished only by the number and position of their dots. Remember that ب has one dot under the line and is pronounced "b", ت has two dots above the line and is pronounced "t" and ن has one dot above the line and is pronounced "n". Always pay close attention to the dots when reading Persian.

PRACTICE 1

Try to recognize these English words in their Persian disguises. Focus on the approximate pronunciation and not necessarily the English spelling. Remember the short and long "a" sounds. The answers are below.

1. انت
2. آنت
3. بت
4. بات
5. کن
6. کت
7. مت
8. تنک

ANSWERS 1

1. ant
2. aunt
3. bat (or bet)
4. bought
5. can
6. cat (or cut)
7. mat
8. tank

PRACTICE 2

Now try to read these real Persian words. The English translation is given next to each word. The correct pronunciations are given in the answers below.

1. بد	(bad)
2. باد	(wind)
3. آب	(water)
4. نان	(bread)
5. بابا	(daddy)
6. بانک	(bank)
7. بدن	(body)
8. دکان	(store / shop)

ANSWERS 2

1. bad
2. bâd
3. âb
4. nân
5. bâbâ
6. bânk
7. badan
8. dokân

UNIT 3 - س, ر, ل, ى

The Persian letter س is pronounced like the "s" sound in "sour" or "Sam" (IPA: /s/). س connects to the previous and the following letters, and therefore has four different forms:

س سـ ـسـ ـس

The letter ر is pronounced with an "r" sound (IPA: /ɾ/). The "r" sound is similar to the "r" sound in the Spanish "caro", but English speakers can use the English "r" sound in "rope" and be understood. ر only connects to the previous letter and has only two forms:

ر ـر

The letter ل is pronounced like the "l" sound in "like" (IPA: /l/). ل connects to the previous and the following letters, and therefore has four different forms:

ل لـ ـلـ ـل

The letter ى is pronounced like the "y" sound in "yellow" when used at the beginning of a word (IPA: /j/). When used in the middle or end of a word, ى is pronounced with a long vowel sound like the "ee" in "bee" or the "i" sound in "spaghetti" (IPA: /i/). ى connects to the previous and the following letters, and therefore has four different forms:

ى یـ ـیـ ـی

TRY NOT TO CONFUSE

The letters ١, and ل can be easy to confuse as they both consist of straight vertical lines. The main difference between these two letters is that ١ does not connect to the following letter, and ل does.

In its initial and medial forms ـبـ resembles ـبـ, ـتـ and ـنـ. As always pay close attention to the number and position of the dots in order to differentiate these letters.

PRACTICE

Try to read these real Persian words. The English translation is given next to each word. The correct pronunciations are given in the answers below.

1. آسمان (sky)
2. سرد (cold)
3. سال (year)
4. باران (rain)
5. لباس (dress)
6. سیب (apple)
7. کلیسا (church)
8. بینی (nose)
9. آبی (blue)
10. یک (one)
11. مرد (man)
12. دریا (sea)

ANSWERS

1. âsmân
2. sard
3. sâl
4. bârân
5. lebâs
6. sib
7. kelisâ
8. bini
9. âbi
10. yek
11. mard
12. daryâ

UNIT 4 - ز, پ, چ, و

The Persian letter ز is pronounced like the "z" sound in "zoo" (IPA: /z/). Like ر, ز only connects to the previous letter and has only two forms:

ز ـز

The letter پ is pronounced like the "p" sound in "pie" (IPA: /p/). پ connects to the previous and following letters and therefore has four forms:

The letter چ is pronounced like the "j" sound in "jam" (IPA: /dʒ/). چ connects to the previous and following letters and has the four following forms:

The letter و is pronounced one of several ways depending on where it is written in the word. At the beginning of a word, or the beginning of a syllable, و is pronounced like the "v" sound in "very" (IPA: /v/). After a consonant, و, is either a long "oo" sound (IPA: /u/), or a long "o" sound (IPA: /o/). و only connects to the preceding letter and not the following letter and so has two forms:

و ـو

11

PRACTICE

Try to read these Persian words. The English translation is given next to each word. The correct pronunciations are given in the answers below.

1. سبز   (green)
2. زرد   (yellow)
3. پنج   (five)
4. پسر   (son)
5. دوست   (friend)
6. کودک   (baby)
7. مسجد   (mosque)
8. جانور   (animal)

ANSWERS

1. sabz
2. zard
3. panj
4. pesar
5. dust
6. kudak
7. masjed
8. jânvar

UNIT 5 - ش, گ, چ, ه

The Persian letter ش is pronounced like the "sh" sound in "she" (IPA: /ʃ/). Although written with two letters in English, "sh" is really one sound and it is written with a single letter in Persian. The "sh" pronunciation will be represented by š in this book. ش connects to the previous and the following letters, and therefore has four different forms:

ش ﺶ ﺸ ﺷ

The letter گ is pronounced like the "g" sound in "good" (IPA: /g/). گ connects to the previous and the following letters, and has the following four forms:

گ ﮓ ﮔ ﮕ

The letter چ is pronounced like the "ch" sound in "church" (IPA: /tʃ/). Although written with two letters in English, "ch" is really one sound and it is written with a single letter in Persian. The "ch" pronunciation will be represented by č in this book. چ connects to the previous and the following letters, and therefore has four different forms:

ﭻ ﭻ ﭼ چ

The letter ه is pronounced like the "h" sound in "house" (IPA: /h/). ه connects to the previous and the following letters, and has four different forms:

ﻪ ﻬ ﻫ ه

When the letter ﻪ is used at the end of the word, it usually signifies the word ends in an "e" sound and the "h" is not pronounced.

13

PRACTICE

Try to read these Persian words. The English translation is given next to each word. The correct pronunciations are given in the answers below.

1. آتش (fire)
2. گل (flower)
3. کوچک (small)
4. هشت (eight)
5. سه (three)
6. موش (mouse)
7. گوش (ear)
8. چشم (eye)
9. چهار (four)
10. بله (yes)
11. پنجره (window)
12. پوشاک (clothing)
13. بزرگ (big)
14. دریاچه (lake)

ANSWERS

1. âtaš
2. gol
3. kučak
4. hašt
5. se
6. muš
7. guš
8. češm
9. čahâr
10. bale
11. panjere
12. pušâk
13. bozorg
14. daryâče

UNIT 6 - ف, خ, ژ, ق, غ

The letter ف is pronounced like the "f" sound in "far" (IPA: /f/).
ف connects to the previous and the following letters, and therefore
has four different forms:

ف ف ف ف

The pronunciation of the Persian letter خ does not exist in English.
It is the "ch" sound in the German "doch" or the "j" sound in the
Spanish "ojos" (IPA: /x/). It is a heavy throat clearing "h" sound.
This letter will be represented as "kh" in the pronunciation in this
book. خ connects to the previous and the following letters, and
therefore has four different forms:

خ خ خ خ

The letter ژ is pronounced like the "s" sound in "pleasure" (IPA:
/ʒ/). This sound will be represented by ž in this book. ژ only
connects to the previous letter and not the following letter and
therefore has two forms:

ژ ژ

The pronunciation of ق also does not exist in English and is
difficult to pronounce at first. It is somewhat similar to the French
"r" sound (IPA: /ɣ/). To practice this sound work with a native
speaker or practice with audio. This letter will be represented as
"q" in the pronunciation in this book. ق connects to the previous
and the following letters, and has the following four forms:

ق ق ق ق

15

In Modern Tehrani Persian, the letter غ is pronounced the same as ق. Careful speakers may differentiate these letters by attempting pronunciations closer to Arabic, but beginners can use the same pronunciation for both letters as that is what most Persian speakers do themselves. This letter will be represented as "gh" in the pronunciation in this book. غ connects to the previous and the following letters, and has these four forms:

غ غـ ـغـ ـغ

PRACTICE

Try to read these Persian words. The English translation is given next to each word. The correct pronunciations are given in the answers below.

1. برف	(snow)
2. سفید	(white)
3. یخ	(ice)
4. خوب	(good)
5. ژانویه	(January)
6. قایق	(boat)
7. قرمز	(red)
8. داغ	(hot)

ANSWERS

1. barf
2. sefid
3. yakh
4. khub
5. žânviye
6. qâyeq
7. qermez
8. dâgh

UNIT 7 - ث, ح, ذ, ع

The four letters introduced in this unit are used mainly to write Arabic loanwords and are much rarer in the Persian language than the letters introduced in the previous units.

The letter ث is pronounced like the "s" sound in "see" (IPA: /s/). It is pronounced the same as س. ث connects to the previous and the following letters, and has four different forms:

ث ﺛ ﺜ ﺚ

The letter ح is pronounced like the "h" sound in "house" (IPA: /h/). It is therefore pronounced the same as ه. ح connects to the previous and the following letters, and has four different forms:

ح ﺤ ﺢ ﺣ

The letter ذ is pronounced like the "z" sound in "zoo" (IPA: /z/). It is therefore pronounced the same as ز. ذ connects to the previous letter but not the following letter and has two different forms:

ذ ﺬ

The letter ع is pronounced with a glottal stop, i.e. a small pause or catch in the throat like in "uh-oh" (IPA: /ʔ/). This pronunciation will be shown as ' (single quotation mark) in this book. ع connects to the previous and the following letters, and has the following four forms:

ع ﻊ ﻌ ﻋ

TRY NOT TO CONFUSE

As we have seen, many letters in Persian have the same shapes and are only distinguished by the number and placement of the dots. It is therefore very important to always pay close attention to the dots when reading Persian.

To review, study the letters below; the letters with the same shapes have been grouped together with their pronunciations shown below the letter.

ب	پ	ت	ث	ن	ی
b	p	t	s	n	y / i

ج	چ	ح	خ
j	č	h	kh

د	ذ
d	z

ر	ز	ژ
r	z	ž

س	ش
s	š

ع	غ
'	gh

ف	ق
f	q

ک	گ
k	g

UNIT 8 - ظ, ط, ض, ص

The four letters introduced in this unit are relatively rare in Persian and are only used to write Arabic loanwords.

The letter ص is pronounced like the "s" sound in "see" (IPA: /s/). It is therefore pronounced the same as س. ص connects to the previous and the following letters, and has four different forms:

ص ـص ـصـ صـ

The letter ض is pronounced like the "z" sound in "zoo" (IPA: /z/). It has the same four forms as ص and is distinguished by the single dot.

The letter ط is pronounced like the "t" sound in "tea" (IPA: /t/). It is therefore pronounced the same as ت. ط connects to the previous and the following letters, and has four different forms:

ط ـط ـطـ طـ

The letter ظ is pronounced like the "z" sound in "zoo" (IPA: /z/). It has the same four forms as ط and is distinguished by the single dot.

Four letters in Persian are all pronounced with a "z" sound. They are ز, ذ, ض and ظ. The first form is by far the most common and the other three forms are only used in Arabic loanwords.

PRACTICE

The letters introduced in units 7 and 8 are less common than the previous letters are they are only used in Arabic loanwords. They are still important, however, as the Persian language uses Arabic words for many of its religious, philosophical, political and scientific words in a similar way that English uses Latin or Greek words.

Iranians also use many names originally from Arabic. Try to read these Persian names to practice the Arabic letters. The correct pronunciations are given in the answers below.

1. محمد

2. احمد

3. علی

4. حمید

ANSWERS

1. Mohammad
2. Ahmad
3. 'Ali
4. Hamid

UNIT 9 - ء, لا

The two symbols introduced in this unit are not technically letters of the Persian alphabet, but are special symbols used in Persian writing in addition to the regular 32 letters of the alphabet.

The symbol ء, called hamze, is used to indicate a glottal stop (IPA: /ʔ/). This pronunciation will be shown as ' (single quotation mark) in this book. The hamze does not connect to other letters but is written "seated" on other letters. In Persian, hamze is never written at the beginning of a word and is silent at the end of a word. Some examples of how ء can be written are:

ئ ؤ ئ ـئـ أ

A special ligature form is written when ل is followed by ا. This form does not change the pronunciation and is merely a special cursive form of the two letters. This special form connects to the previous letter but not to the following letter and has two forms:

لا ـلا

PRACTICE

Try to read these Persian words. The English translation is given next to each word. The correct pronunciations are given in the answers below.

1. ژوئن   (June)
2. ژوئیه   (July)
3. کلاه   (hat)

ANSWERS

1. žu'an
2. žu'iye
3. kolâh

UNIT 10 - REVIEW

PRACTICE 1

Review the previous lessons by reading these real Persian place names. The correct pronunciations are given in the Answers below.

1. تهران
2. مشهد
3. اصفهان
4. تبریز
5. شیراز
6. دریای مازندران
7. خلیج فارس
8. البرز
9. آزاد کوه
10. دریاچه نمک

ANSWERS 1

1. Tehrân
2. Mašhad
3. Isfahân
4. Tabriz
5. Širâz
6. Daryâ-e Mâzandarân (Caspian Sea)
7. Khalij-e Fârs (Persian Gulf)
8. Alborz
9. Âzâd Kuh
10. Daryâče-ye Namak

PRACTICE 2

Review what you have learned in this book by reading the Persian surnames below. The correct pronunciations are given in the Answers below.

1. خمینی
2. روحانی
3. احمدی‌نژاد
4. خاتمی
5. فرهادی
6. رفسنجانی
7. خامنه‌ای
8. مهاجرانی
9. افشار
10. جبرانی

ANSWERS 2

1. Khomeini
2. Ruhâni
3. Ahmedinežâd
4. Khâtami
5. Farhâdi
6. Rafsanjâni
7. Khâmenei
8. Mohâjerâni
9. Âfšâr
10. Jobrâni

PERSIAN ALPHABET

Letter	Pronunciation
ا / آ	[a], [â], [o], [e]
ب	[b]
پ	[p]
ت	[t]
ث	[s]
ج	[j]
چ	[č]
ح	[h]
خ	[kh]
د	[d]
ذ	[z]
ر	[r]
ز	[z]
ژ	[ž]
س	[s]

ش	[š]
ص	[s]
ض	[z]
ط	[t]
ظ	[z]
ع	[']
غ	[gh]
ف	[f]
ق	[q]
ک	[k]
گ	[g]
ل	[l]
م	[m]
ن	[n]
ه	[h]
و	[v], [u], [o]
ی	[y], [i]

GLOSSARY – THEMATIC ORDER

ANIMALS

جانور	[jânvar]	animal
سگ	[sag]	dog
گربه	[gorbe]	cat
ماهی	[mâhi]	fish
پرنده	[parande]	bird
گاو	[gâv]	cow
خوک	[khuk]	pig
موش	[muš]	mouse
اسب	[asb]	horse

PEOPLE

شخص	[šakhs]	person
مادر	[mâdar]	mother
مامان	[mâmân]	mommy / mama
پدر	[pedar]	father
بابا	[bâbâ]	daddy / papa
پسر	[pesar]	son / boy
دختر	[dokhtar]	daughter / girl
برادر	[barâdar]	brother
خواهر	[khâhar]	sister
دوست	[dust]	friend
مرد	[mard]	man
زن	[zan]	woman
بچه	[bačče]	child
کودک	[kudak]	baby

TRANSPORTATION

قطار	[qatâr]	train
هواپیما	[havâpeymâ]	airplane
ماشین	[mâšin]	car (automobile)
دوچرخه	[dočarkhe]	bicycle
اتوبوس	[otobus]	bus
قایق	[qâyeq]	boat

LOCATION

شهر	[šahr]	city
خانه	[khâne]	house
خیابان	[khiyâbân]	street
فرودگاه	[forudgâh]	airport
هتل	[hotel]	hotel
رستوران	[restorân]	restaurant
مدرسه	[madrese]	school
دانشگاه	[dânešgâ]	university
پارک	[park]	park
دکان	[dokân]	store / shop
بیمارستان	[bimârestân]	hospital
کلیسا	[kelisâ]	church
مسجد	[masjed]	mosque
کشور	[kešvar]	country (state)
بانک	[bânk]	bank
بازار	[bâzâr]	market

HOME

میز	[miz]	table
صندلی	[sandali]	chair
پنجره	[panjere]	window
در	[dar]	door
کتاب	[ketâb]	book

CLOTHING

پوشاک	[pušâk]	clothing
کلاه	[kolâh]	hat
لباس	[lebâs]	dress
پیراهن	[pirâhan]	shirt
شلوار	[šalvâr]	pants
کفش	[kafš]	shoe

BODY

بدن	[badan]	body
سر	[sar]	head
روی	[ruy]	face
مو	[mu]	hair
چشم	[češm]	eye
دهان	[dahân]	mouth
بینی	[bini]	nose
گوش	[guš]	ear
دست	[dast]	hand / arm
پا	[pâ]	foot / leg
دل	[del]	heart
خون	[khun]	blood
استخوان	[ostokhân]	bone
ریش	[riš]	beard

MISCELLANEOUS

| بله | [bale] | yes |
| نه | [na] | no |

FOOD & DRINK

غذا	[ghazâ]	food
گوشت	[gušt]	meat
نان	[nân]	bread
پنیر	[panir]	cheese
سیب	[sib]	apple
آب	[âb]	water
آبجو	[âb-jow]	beer
شراب	[šarâb]	wine
قهوه	[qahve]	coffee
چای	[čây]	tea
شیر	[šir]	milk
صبحانه	[sobhâne]	breakfast
ناهار	[nâhâr]	lunch
شام	[šâm]	dinner

COLORS

رنگ	[rang]	color
قرمز	[qermez]	red
آبی	[âbi]	blue
سبز	[sabz]	green
زرد	[zard]	yellow
سیاه	[siyâh]	black
سفید	[sefid]	white

NATURE

دریا	[daryâ]	sea
رود	[rud]	river
دریاچه	[daryâče]	lake
کوه	[kuh]	mountain
باران	[bârân]	rain
برف	[barf]	snow
درخت	[derakht]	tree
گل	[gol]	flower
خورشید	[khoršid]	sun
ماه	[mâh]	moon
باد	[bâd]	wind
آسمان	[âsmân]	sky
آتش	[âtaš]	fire
یخ	[yakh]	ice

ADJECTIVES

بزرگ	[bozorg]	big
کوچک	[kučak]	small
خوب	[khub]	good
بد	[bad]	bad
داغ	[dâgh]	hot
سرد	[sard]	cold
ارزان	[arzân]	cheap
گران	[gerân]	expensive
خوشحال	[khošhâl]	happy
غمگین	[ghamgin]	sad

31

NUMBERS

یک	[yek]	one
دو	[do]	two
سه	[se]	three
چهار	[čahâr]	four
پنج	[panj]	five
شش	[šeš]	six
هفت	[haft]	seven
هشت	[hašt]	eight
نه	[no]	nine
ده	[dah]	ten

TIME

روز	[ruz]	day
ماه	[mâh]	month
سال	[sâl]	year
ساعت	[sâ'at]	hour
امروز	[emruz]	today
فردا	[fardâ]	tomorrow
دیروز	[diruz]	yesterday

DAYS OF THE WEEK

یکشنبه	[yek-šanbe]	Sunday
دوشنبه	[do-šanbe]	Monday
سه‌شنبه	[se-šanbe]	Tuesday
چهارشنبه	[čahâr-šanbe]	Wednesday
پنج‌شنبه	[panj-šanbe]	Thursday
جمعه	[jom'e]	Friday
شنبه	[šanbe]	Saturday

32

MONTHS (GREGORIAN)

ژانویه	[žânviye]	January
فوریه	[fevriye]	February
مارس	[mars]	March
آوریل	[âvril]	April
مه	[me]	May
ژوئن	[žu'an]	June
ژوئیه	[žu'iye]	July
اوت	[ut]	August
سپتامبر	[septâmbr]	September
اکتبر	[oktobr]	October
نوامبر	[novâmbr]	November
دسامبر	[desâmbr]	December

MONTHS (IRANIAN)

فروردین	[farvardin]	Farvardin
اردیبهشت	[ordibehešt]	Ordibehesht
خرداد	[khordâd]	Khordad
تیر	[tir]	Tir
امرداد	[amordâd]	Amordad
شهریور	[šahrivar]	Shahrivar
مهر	[mehr]	Mehr
آبان	[âbân]	Aban
آذر	[âzar]	Azar
دی	[dey]	Dey
بهمن	[bahman]	Bahman
اسفند	[esfand]	Esfand

33

PROPER NAMES

ایران	[irân]	Iran
ایرانی	[irâni]	Iranian (person)
تهران	[tehrân]	Tehran
افغانستان	[afghânestân]	Afghanistan
کابل	[kâbul]	Kabul
فارسی	[fârsi]	Persian (Farsi)

GLOSSARY – ALPHABETICAL ORDER

_ آ _

آب	[âb]	water
آبان	[âbân]	8th month (Iranian)
آبجو	[âb-jow]	beer
آبی	[âbi]	blue
آتش	[âtaš]	fire
آذر	[âzar]	9th month (Iranian)
آسمان	[âsmân]	sky
آوریل	[âvril]	April

_ ا _

اتوبوس	[otobus]	bus
اردیبهشت	[ordibehešt]	2nd month (Iranian)
ارزان	[arzân]	cheap
اسب	[asb]	horse
استخوان	[ostokhân]	bone
اسفند	[esfand]	12th month (Iran.)
افغانستان	[afghânestân]	Afghanistan
اکتبر	[oktobr]	October
امرداد	[amordâd]	5th month (Iranian)
امروز	[emruz]	today
اوت	[ut]	August
ایران	[irân]	Iran
ایرانی	[irâni]	Iranian (person)

– ب –

بابا	[bâbâ]	daddy / papa
باد	[bâd]	wind
باران	[bârân]	rain
بازار	[bâzâr]	market
بانک	[bânk]	bank
بچه	[bačče]	child
بد	[bad]	bad
بدن	[badan]	body
برادر	[barâdar]	brother
برف	[barf]	snow
بزرگ	[bozorg]	big
بله	[bale]	yes
بهمن	[bahman]	11th month (Iran.)
بیمارستان	[bimârestân]	hospital
بینی	[bini]	nose

– پ –

پا	[pâ]	foot / leg
پارک	[park]	park
پدر	[pedar]	father
پرنده	[parande]	bird
پسر	[pesar]	son / boy
پنج	[panj]	five
پنجره	[panjere]	window
پنجشنبه	[panj-šanbe]	Thursday
پنیر	[panir]	cheese
پوشاک	[pušâk]	clothing
پیراهن	[pirâhan]	shirt

ـ ت ـ

| تهران | [tehrân] | Tehran |
| تیر | [tir] | 4th month (Iranian) |

ـ ج ـ

| جانور | [jânvar] | animal |
| جمعه | [jom'e] | Friday |

ـ چ ـ

چای	[čây]	tea
چشم	[češm]	eye
چهار	[čahâr]	four
چهارشنبه	[čahâr-šanbe]	Wednesday

ـ خ ـ

خانه	[khâne]	house
خرداد	[khordâd]	3rd month (Iranian)
خواهر	[khâhar]	sister
خوب	[khub]	good
خورشید	[khoršid]	sun
خوشحال	[khošhâl]	happy
خوک	[khuk]	pig
خون	[khun]	blood
خیابان	[khiyâbân]	street

ـ د ـ

داغ	[dâgh]	hot
دانشگاه	[dânešgâ]	university
دختر	[dokhtar]	daughter / girl
در	[dar]	door
درخت	[derakht]	tree
دریا	[daryâ]	sea
دریاچه	[daryâče]	lake
دسامبر	[desâmbr]	December
دست	[dast]	hand / arm
دکان	[dokân]	store / shop
دل	[del]	heart
ده	[dah]	ten
دهان	[dahân]	mouth
دو	[do]	two
دوچرخه	[dočarkhe]	bicycle
دوست	[dust]	friend
دوشنبه	[do-šanbe]	Monday
دی	[dey]	12th month (Iran.)
دیروز	[diruz]	yesterday

ـ ر ـ

رستوران	[restorân]	restaurant
رنگ	[rang]	color
رود	[rud]	river
روز	[ruz]	day
روی	[ruy]	face
ریش	[riš]	beard

– ز –

زرد	[zard]	yellow
زن	[zan]	woman

– ژ –

ژانویه	[žânviye]	January
ژوئن	[žu'an]	June
ژوئیه	[žu'iye]	July

– س –

ساعت	[sâ'at]	hour
سال	[sâl]	year
سبز	[sabz]	green
سپتامبر	[septâmbr]	September
سر	[sar]	head
سرد	[sard]	cold
سفید	[sefid]	white
سگ	[sag]	dog
سه	[se]	three
سه‌شنبه	[se-šanbe]	Tuesday
سیاه	[siyâh]	black
سیب	[sib]	apple

‫ش‬ ‫–‬ ‫–‬

‫شام‬	[šâm]	dinner
‫شخص‬	[šakhs]	person
‫شراب‬	[šarâb]	wine
‫شش‬	[šeš]	six
‫شلوار‬	[šalvâr]	pants
‫شنبه‬	[šanbe]	Saturday
‫شهر‬	[šahr]	city
‫شهریور‬	[šahrivar]	6th month (Iran.)
‫شیر‬	[šir]	milk

‫ص‬ ‫–‬ ‫–‬

| ‫صبحانه‬ | [sobhâne] | breakfast |
| ‫صندلی‬ | [sandali] | chair |

‫غ‬ ‫–‬ ‫–‬

| ‫غذا‬ | [ghazâ] | food |
| ‫غمگین‬ | [ghamgin] | sad |

‫ف‬ ‫–‬ ‫–‬

‫فارسی‬	[fârsi]	Persian (Farsi)
‫فردا‬	[fardâ]	tomorrow
‫فرودگاه‬	[forudgâh]	airport
‫فروردین‬	[farvardin]	1st month (Iranian)
‫فوریه‬	[fevriye]	February

40

– ق –

قایق	[qâyeq]	boat
قرمز	[qermez]	red
قطار	[qatâr]	train
قهوه	[qahve]	coffee

– ک –

کابل	[kâbul]	Kabul
کتاب	[ketâb]	book
کشور	[kešvar]	country (state)
کفش	[kafš]	shoe
کلاه	[kolâh]	hat
کلیسا	[kelisâ]	church
کوچک	[kučak]	small
کودک	[kudak]	baby
کوه	[kuh]	mountain

– گ –

گاو	[gâv]	cow
گران	[gerân]	expensive
گربه	[gorbe]	cat
گل	[gol]	flower
گوش	[guš]	ear
گوشت	[gušt]	meat

– ل –

لباس	[lebâs]	dress

– م –

مادر	[mâdar]	mother
مارس	[mars]	March
ماشین	[mâšin]	car (automobile)
مامان	[mâmân]	mommy / mama
ماه	[mâh]	moon / month
ماهی	[mâhi]	fish
مدرسه	[madrese]	school
مرد	[mard]	man
مسجد	[masjed]	mosque
مه	[me]	May
مهر	[mehr]	7th month (Iranian)
مو	[mu]	hair
موش	[muš]	mouse
میز	[miz]	table

– ن –

نان	[nân]	bread
ناهار	[nâhâr]	lunch
نه	[na]	no
نه	[no]	nine
نوامبر	[novâmbr]	November

هتل	[hotel]	hotel
هشت	[hašt]	eight
هفت	[haft]	seven
هواپیما	[havâpeymâ]	airplane

— ى —

یخ	[yakh]	ice
یک	[yek]	one
یکشنبه	[yek-šanbe]	Sunday

Other language learning titles available from Wolfedale Press:

Learn to Read Arabic in 5 Days
Learn to Read Armenian in 5 Days
Learn to Read Bulgarian in 5 Days
Learn to Read Georgian in 5 Days
Learn to Read Greek in 5 Days
Learn to Read Modern Hebrew in 5 Days
Learn to Read Russian in 5 Days
Learn to Read Ukrainian in 5 Days